"In *The Days You Bring*, we walk the 'long walk' with Recinos through the barrio's streets, weeping unabashedly for its 'crucified people' and left to contemplate the 'horrifying obscenity of forgetfulness.' Yet so, too, do we revel in its subtle raptures and improbable blossoms. Against the 'thick silence' of an indifferent world and the 'pious white lies' of history, *The Days You Bring* asks us, Can you hear the barrio's song? Its canto and hymns? Its 'unanswered prayers'?"

—Éric Morales-Franceschini,
University of Georgia

"This is a magnificent work of art. . . . These poems urgently reprimand white Americans for their belief in a God who sanctions a racist capitalism that can't afford to care about the barrio, the jail, and the border. Recinos is 'carrying this cold / country in my brown body' with ecstatic grief shot through with grace restored to its name."

—Katie Ford,
University of California, Riverside

"I have often thought that American presidents should add a poet or two to their cabinets. It seems to me that along with financiers, generals, lawyers, physicians, and scientists, a bard should be part of this assembly of wisdom for a nation. Harold Recinos is an operatic poet for our time. In his new collection, he tells Americans exactly what they need to hear right now—full blast—about the life we share so they can change it."

—Lori Marie Carlson-Hijuelos,
author of *Voices in First Person: Reflections on Latino Identity*

"The impassioned poems of protest in *The Days You Bring* contribute to poetry's social justice tradition, offering us closely observed and tender chronicles of the innocent who suffer. Recinos's outpourings of torrential rage and sorrow are leavened by finely grained moments of soft grace."

—JOY CASTRO,
University of Nebraska-Lincoln

"In this collection of truth-telling poetry, Harold Recinos weeps with love for the dehumanized and marginalized of society. He laments over injustice, yet he does more than this. He dreams of a more luminous future and hopes amid human hurts until he can say in the end, literally, 'Amen!' If you desire to be lit by the fire of a just God, read this book. These poems are from the tongue of a prophet."

—LUKE A. POWERY,
Duke University

The Days You Bring

The Days You Bring

HAROLD J. RECINOS

RESOURCE *Publications* • Eugene, Oregon

THE DAYS YOU BRING

Resource Publications
An Imprint of Wipf and Stock Publishers
199 W. 8th Ave., Suite 3
Eugene, OR 97401

www.wipfandstock.com

PAPERBACK ISBN: 978-1-6667-3839-1
HARDCOVER ISBN: 978-1-6667-9903-3
EBOOK ISBN: 978-1-6667-9904-0

June 20, 2022 8:05 AM

Contents

BARRIO

I never tire of the city
with scented wind that
sobs some nights. I love
to see the people on her
sidewalks when the moon
shines. I stop to learn the
name of the winos sleeping
church steps beneath God's
heaven. I am in love with
those rare moments when
butterflies dance their way
across the busy streets to
tell me life is not dark and
cold.

BELOVED

this morning there was scarcely
a sound on the streets, the clouds
floated over the rooftops dropping
a little rain and I could see almost
to the East River. I walked down
the sidewalk passing the building
where w. h. Auden lived that now
sits beside a Pizza Shop popular with
the junkies and winos who never tire
of sitting in the cold light of Thompkins
Square Park. on the way to the river,
tender memories came to me, I waved
to the Brazilian Pentecostal preacher
sweeping the sidewalk in front of his
storefront church and smiled at the sight
of a rather large man walking with his
Chihuahua on a long leach as pigeons
flew above the dog's head. I thought
about the stuff we live with everyday
on the Alphabet streets, the grocery
store owners who left their enchanted
island many years ago and still had a
look in their eyes of not getting what
they really wanted. I wondered how
many of us in this neighborhood sat
down in the odd hours of dark nights

to write letters to America about being
beloved in a country that says it has
too little to give?

THE WOMEN

the women who arrived
two months ago are in the
corner grocery store getting
a few things for an evening
meal with children who have
already picked up lots of new
world English. they are at the
counter paying Mr. Perez who
owns the bodega with money that
trembles in their hands like it
was something to fear. the teen
stocking shelves with Goya beans
on one of the aisles has no idea
what it was like in the faraway
places these women fled, why
the woman dressed in black
weeps unannounced when she sees
green legal tender with the words
in God We Trust that paid for death
to come prematurely to a husband
running away from soldiers. they
make money cleaning private homes
that never ask them for documents,
makes them stand up against a wall,
and threatens them with jail time. yet,
the little cash they earn causes them

to shiver, weep, and sometimes pray
for it to buy enough food and cover
the week's rent so they can keep
a roof over children's heads in a
world demanding their lives.

RIVER JORDAN

I weep for the men, women and
children murdered in harsh time,
no longer smelling the sweetness
of each fleeting day, lost forever
in a darkness that will never taste
love, removed from the world by
the devils who delightfully lock
gas chamber doors and mocked
by the malignant fools who
spend their time imagining the
triumph of injustice. I weep for
a society that repeatedly elects
lies shown in churches, schools,
courts, government and ordinary
streets with torrential contempt
for truth and flattery for those who
choke the witnesses against hate
and deceit to death. I weep for the
thin light of democracy that is stuffed
with the same bullshit the latest version
of sanitized history books use in schools
to refute the horrors of terrorized and slain
people. I weep without any tears left for
America's denial of memory and for the
day crucified people will at last see God's
messenger of mercy cover the world full of
hate with a blanket of flowers!

FRIENDS

my friends enjoy windy nights
on city park benches nodding
to the faint sound of children
in their last half-hour of play.
they spend hours talking about
the girl without parents, brothers
lost in wars, mangoes that fell
at the oddest hours and dreams
touched only by God. my friends
laugh about plastic slip covered
furniture, doors that open to dark
spaces, the beauty of dark-skinned
selves and the idea of a civilized
whiteness. my friends are sleeping
in the subways, the flop houses, the
park, the bus stations, the tenement
roofs and stairwells bemoaning the
fascist use of race, the contempt for
Spanish and the power of Providence
imagined by murder, rape and theft
of land. my friends drink on the stoop
saying life is not a long misery in
the dark, the different, the exile, the
hated, the angry and the non-English
speaking siblings of Christ.

SILENCE

we talked, painted messages on
walls and marched to keep days

beautiful for our children sold on
the idea the world is worth it. we

gathered in winter apartments
beside kitchen stoves warming

ourselves with stories that have
burned in us. we recalled the tired

backs of mothers trying to carry us
to the promised land, wondering

why the Lord no longer lingers
with the Spanglish people in the

slums and tired of seeing sons and
daughters treated like less. we sat

on the stoop saying all the things
not allowed in school, refusing to

hold our tongues, denouncing with
words taken from two languages the

gods of society who allow children
to hold guns instead of books. we

confessed that in a nation with so
much police brutality and too many

churches singing to a God who does
not see the wretched on earth, no one

cares about Oscar Romero or Martin
Luther King, and billionaires are adored

on the covers of magazines.

TINY HAT

I once saw an old man with
a fiddle in the alley behind
Westchester Avenue in the
company of the cutest tiny
dressed monkey the kids at
their windows had ever seen.
it danced, tumbled, clapped
and gracefully took off its hat
then climbed the fire escapes
with a little bowl to collect
audience coins and even a few
green bills. after many years,
I had forgotten how beautiful
was the sound of laughter in
the unfrequented alley where
poor children play.

LOVE

love in a time of illness
opens the gates, breaks
down the walls, sells all
hate, hushes crying and
brings dreams alive with
a simple kiss. in these times,
love enfolds us, has us cling
to each other on earth with
thirsty lips, stirs the finite
frame with heaven and feeds
the hidden sacred flame. love
in a time of illness is tender
with the faltering voice, warm
with the sorrowing heart and
always a kindle of hope. love
is an unpredictable emotion
rushing like a river to wash
us clean and cut canyons in
our fragile soul.

THE VILLAGE

we live in a place
that knows nothing
about walls and doors
though the air becomes
heavier each day and
Jesus is met on empty
lots hiding in trash and
sleeping in cardboard
huts with poor Puerto
Ricans not accounted
for in the evening news
or white metaphysics.
we are the people you
tell jokes about in cocktail
parties, cross the street to
avoid in big cities, never
embraced in church and who
chew beneath the evening
light the same bread. we
are those who hang from a
thread unseen, earning petty
wages that decomposes all
hope and who marched with
Martin the day he gave the I
have a dream speech. we are
the people who still show up

on Sunday to listen with tired
faces, grieving hearts and
decaying faith to the same
old crumbling good news
that only offers fives loaves
of rotted bread and two dead
fish. we are the people of the
block wondering what will
become of us, our Spanglish
kids and Black and Brown
hands around here carrying
la biblia.

CONTAINER

the little boy went
to the kitchen and
opened the fridge.
he reached for the
container of milk
and drank it save
for the tiny pool
left to be shaken.
he did not tell the
hungry souls in the
house the milk was
delicious and filled
his empty stomach
quite well.

BEDTIME STORIES

I fetched a book at bedtime to read
to each of my children over the years
recalling whenever at the end of each
chapter years spent in libraries to get
out of the cold when homeless. I read
C.S. Lewis' Chronicles of Narnia again
and again, showing my kids stories like
this lead us to the places where enchanted
fruit hangs. the nightly ritual was the
most beautiful off-the-record prayer my
kids enjoyed with me and still I say with
trembling lips give me more time. they
are grown now but know how to trust the
darkness when they lay their sleepy heads
for a rest that takes them into dreams of
timeless love. I often wonder why the years
ran so swiftly and then I whisper their names
in the odd hours of the morning when the stars
are steadily shining to caste spells in many
parts and to help the dark see.

SPANISH HARLEM

I tread down Lenox Avenue
with my nose in a book of
Langston's poems that are
never sped read by me. I lift
my eyes to cross the street
still heading toward the East
River convinced every word
in Crossing Jordan was meant
for my old man who never
crossed water into a land of
dreams. I walk down to Third
Avenue and make my way to
Spanish Harlem where a whole
lot of people look like me and I
tell my beloved Langston in a soft
voice I am not alone. I find a
stoop to take a seat and see some
Mexican masons on the other
side of the street on scaffolding
laying bricks in a building that
will have apartments for sale
and I am confident not one of
them will build a border Wall
despised by God. I lean into Langston
a little more to think about America
mad with hate and absurd terror
for us.

HOLY WATER

America has tried to kill me since
the day I was born in a cheap city
hospital where Puerto Rican mothers
mourned together and shared wisdom
about how to train kids to survive. it
did not take long to learn the grammar
of this ancient story, to run faster than
knives chasing me and flee the swinging
batons of errant cops that loved nothing
more than to play baseball on the block
with spic heads. the boys I use to fly kites
with on the rooftops were pursued by the
same assassin, some of them are already
resting beneath the earth and others learned
to carry knives bigger than their forearms
to slice up the world that had thousands of
reasons for them to leave it. sometimes, in
quiet moments of rest, I have shouted out
to Maya that on the block freed birds do not
ever leap into the wind and all the songs we
have learned are about the ball, chain, whip
and gallows. America has been praying too
long for people like me to be battered and
lowered into undocumented graves but we
keep sipping Holy water and never stop
cutting down the lynching trees!

HOLY BASTARD

God of migrants,
you look upon the
Brown faces of new
arrivals and say their
names in Spanish.
God of children too
weak in cages with
faces lost to churches
keep them from the
white hand of death
on American soil.
God of travelers with
dreams, escape artists
of violence, battered
women in the world
and raped teen girls
find them. God who
bleeds like migrants,
suffers like refugees,
howls in the desserts
and whispers the stories
the world does not want
to hear look upon your
Brown faces with kindness
and deliver them to the
promised land. God of

songs in exile, tell the
wicked of this land these
Brown bodies like Jesus
will be set free and put
truth in their souls unlike
preachers making money
with your words and blessing
wealthy thieves and drifting
human beings who dance to
the music played beside the new
lynching trees.

RESURRECTION

we sat on the stoop
watching a couple of

dogs rummage through
garbage wondering out

loud about the place the
resurrected line up, the

graffiti they must come
up with, whether it is a

space where sun shines,
the ocean is carried in the

wind, the Puerto Rican
girls fancy skipping rope

like on the block, widows
shed black dresses, inner

city soldiers see the return
of lost limbs, old men never

tire and tears are swept away
never to be dropped. Tito wondered

whether or not you would have
a better time in that place by

going around the block spray
painting passages of scripture

on the walls of banks, stores and
the tenements that did not rent

an apartment to his mother, Cuca.
I confessed not having an answer

for him, then shared when children
run games on the streets and the

storefront churches are bustling
with the noise of Spanish sung

hymns Eden abounds down here
and the path to the resurrection

line in heaven is clearer than the river
that watered the garden in Eden.

LIVING

for months these boys walked
in search of a destiny in a new
country. they have worn smiles
step after step, floated the river
on truck inner tubes, thought up
a personal trip vocabulary and in
unison sang of the world that just
pushed them into exile. there will
be no use looking for the names of
village streets in the city that awaits
them and it will take time to begin
to understand others who will give
orders in work places in a language
that might as well be wordless. who
knows like the immense beauty of
the moon for lovers and the sweetest
dreams ever imagined while lighting
a candle to la Virgen de Guadalupe
freedom will finally come for them
and they will soon stand on their own
two feet.

HOLY SPIRIT

they have talked about the
Holy Spirit like nothing could
be better understood though it
has lost hold of most of us. the
curtain was raised on it in places
that have too much to say and no
bright light, parting of clouds or
deep voice said a thing. we have
instinctively raised questions about
it, wished it would strain itself to
help us exist with the daily struggle
and open its lips to speak to us in
Spanish and broken English just to
convince us it exists. you know, I
ran into little Papo on Longfellow
Avenue, he was still waiting for the
Holy Spirit to toss him a rescue rope
from heaven to resurrect his near dead
heart. little Papo would much rather light
candles to save money on electricity in
his tiny apartment than in the local Catholic
church that once washed his head with water
like something big happened for the Holy
Spirit to witness. little Papo told me once
church is just a chatter room and the divine
spirit never attends the fucken Mass.

HUCKLEBERRY FINN

they told him Mark Twain's fiction
would be irresistible even in Spanish
translation. by the time he descended
into the Big city on an eastern shore
he wondered about the claim and how
The Adventures of Huckleberry Finn
that launched so many literary careers
was a grand American story about race
relations imaging the moral predicament
essentially of the white struggle over what
to do about a runaway slave instead of a Black
man's fight for freedom. he concluded the
big lesson that his adopted country needed
to learn from Finn was how to shut up and
listen to the voices howling in a social order
dead set against equality. in the long passing
years in his new English-speaking world, he
thought the American classic demanded a kick
off the pedestal especially for using the most
powerful racial epithet in the English language
213 times. in time, he developed a deep liking
for Ralph Ellison's Invisible Man that resonated
with his Puerto Rican soul and agreed with Ellison
that Twain fitted Jim into a white distortion of slavery.
damn, America he thought still sells Black lives and

dark human beings down the river for laughs and Twain
in translation is just a tall tale about the offer of freedom
in a white world.

WALKING ON FIFTH

let's follow the clouds down
Fifth Avenue, detour through
a few alleys and places we have
never seen. let's walk imagining
home is near, hiding inside each
Spanish word, hearing them call
us from sidewalk trees and the noon
church bells tolling. when the wind
rises and blows North on Fifth feel it
gently touch you without whispering
the name of this city and let it say we
are not alien visitors here. take in the
smells telling stories, have a good look
at the old arrivals that settled generations
ago and have forgotten not to speak in
English and remember why you did not
arrive on Ellis Island.

THE GUIDE

I will guide you on these
concrete streets to the East
River banks, pass the corners
with stammering tongues and
the stoops with fallen Puerto
Rican kids. I will walk you the
length of the slums until your
eyes open and you weep for
the world shared with you. we
will stroll pass tents set up on
a lot beside a church that rings
bells to an empty heaven, collect
Spanish words you never once
heard that speak of the dark in
every direction. I will guide you
all the way to the projects at the
end of Avenue D and wait for you
to ask is this what happens to the
people who spend every hour in
prayer and pay dearly for white
sins?

DREAM

born in a former colonial
city that passed through a
number of cultural hands
that finally was made into
a home for a mother who
came from a pretty village
of Brown girls has left me
singing salsa, sipping café
con leche and wondering
long about the things hope
foresees. I have a dream
has remained the great line
haunting the sobering streets
familiar to people like me
in the barrio who look high
and low for the land of the
beautiful, hear police sirens
rush down the streets and stand
around the ambulances picking
up fallen little kids. I wonder
about the weekly lines in church
and the God who allegedly blesses
those who hold tightly to dreams
in a world where daring to have them
makes you suspect and illegal.

PASSAGES

you do not understand Spanish
and that makes our words float

down American streets, drown
in the wells of democracy and

sink in the sludge of English
only ears. though you see us on

a daily basis, we are no less than
the disappeared, noise that rattles

the dark, abandoned lifeless
bodies on urban streets and the

people white society depends on
to achieve anything. we are the

names written on your bombs,
the truth you laugh at during the

armored parade, the stain on the
Capitols steps and rejectors of

the stench of your American
God. we are the people who do

not forget to die on the border,
in the alleys, rooftops, rivers,

oceans, tenements, fields, jails
and each other's arms in places

fled. we are the people the star
spangled banner never seems to

tire of bleeding! we are the sounds
of those who will the sweet life you

will always hear in the dark!

WHITE CRIME

I catch stories of
white criminals
in the news, the
elected officials
who break the law
and stay safe and
free. I catch the
sight of the white
men and women
who have left the
nation scarred and
Black and Brown
humanity feeling
next. I see white
institutions hollering
up a storm, pointing
the finger of blame
and doing nothing
to extract the poison
from the country's
ill veins. I know the
names of these white
privileged gangsters
doing the crimes but
not the time. white
lies all around that
never die!

TOMORROW

I was walking down first avenue
by myself, made the sign of the
cross when passing the big old
Catholic church, felt a strong cold
wind against my face and thought
we've been crossing the Jordan
almost every day on these streets
and not once found the promised
land or the dreams rolling around
in our heads. the old man I ran into
on Avenue B carrying a fish beneath
his arm whispered the same tired
words that miracles are on the other
side of the water that doesn't flow
down here.

ROSE WINDOWS

the gated churches with colorful
Rose Windows imaging a white
Jesus nailed to a tree who never
moans lie about the sound of life
around here. the winos who sleep
it off on the church steps the cops
sometimes drag away by the neck
who mutter Spanish have known a
very different Savior lying beside
them in the dark. sometimes children
play on the sidewalk in front of this
God they have never known shouting
and laughing about the living paradise
they have touched. I want to sit here
on the church steps getting blessed by
these kids though the world hardens
and the hollering is unheard inside the
big old church.

THE LIGHT

morning is a time to see
with the sounds of birds
whistling in the wind, to
hear migrant footsteps that
approach from the South,
observe the elderly couples
in old gym clothes walking
the sidewalks and children
come out to play. in the Perez
grocery store old women are
already buying spices for an
evening meal, the disabled
vets set up their domino table,
even Dante would look around
the block and find no evidence
of hell. a group of young girls
sit perfectly still on the stoop of
a building with boarded windows
on the first floor, they look at me
leaning on the fire hydrant and I
smile aware that everything does
not end.

SPANISH HARLEM

by the time I was ten it was
clear to me this country did
not want to share its dream.
its crime is it keeps telling
me to go home when I am
already here and have become
an expert at watching the fires
it sets. the bodies have been
falling in my barrio and no one
beyond its boundaries has ever
taken the time to notice and I
suspect even a great theologian
would sit on the neighborhood
church steps and only see city
sparrows hopping on sidewalks,
instead of human beings. by the
time I could write in English it
was clear to me too many people
in the country did not see the barrio
in the same light and Spanglish
America with its tropical sounds,
hands, faces and feet should just
disappear—every day my people
are reduced, clipped and lynched
you see for calling this country
home!

SONG

I want to make my way to
the speaking corner to find old

friends who can still remember
carefree days to make a necklace

of them to wear in the places that
never look their way. I want to visit

the Valencia Bakery before dying
for bread with butter, feel Autumn

breezes coming from every direction,
listen to the subway overhead on its

way downtown with moonlike eyes
staring out door windows and say a

prayer for those lying under earth
too young. I want to stop on a long

walk in front of a drifting piece of
newspaper the wind allowed to rest

on the street, read its small print and
be reminded of all the good news the

world oversees. I want to walk north
to the flowered park carrying this cold

country in my brown body and whisper
what is it like to feel equal and free

of chains that make us stutter until
hushed? I want to reach into my pocket

and find boney barrio hands leading
me away from the years of massacre,

ruined children's lives and back to
the promise of paradise.

COLORS

I wonder about watching the
news today that reports after
sponsors selling car insurance
that a Black man is serving life
in prison in a deep South jail
for stealing nine dollars in a
world that likes to keep closing
death in on him in a cage. I don't
know how to escape the aching
in my soul hearing a white cop
who claimed the life of a Black
father got away with twenty-two
years for murder! tell me what
time do you expect heaven will
stone the hell out of racist cops,
lynching judges and a society
that beats us, hangs us, jails us,
hates us and still dares to pray
for peace? tell me when for
heaven's sake will you see the
bloody scars on our backs, weep
for our dead in cheap pine boxes
and confess hundreds of years of
white hate? tell me how long must
we look at blood-stained streets, gasp
for air, put photos up in jail cells
and recite unanswered prayers?

INFERNO

something keeps us silent
on this storied land with

far too many anonymous
dead. something makes us

afraid to speak the sounds
we brought on this piece

of earth where people fall
apart. something in the towns,

villages, cities and old farms
prefer to allow ignorance to

spread like rot on floor boards.
the time will come to look

through the eyes of children
who long to absorb America

full of kindness and vicious
white supremacy to drop dead.

something in us refuses to weep
shamelessly about the shut lips

saying nothing about the sweet
chariots that will swing low to

perish the slingers of shit whose
disfigured souls are knotted by

darkness.

CAFÉ CON LECHE

I remember that day in the
café when the world was a
little less fractured, the fires
from the civil war were out,
life felt slightly fuller and we
wanted time to march for an
eternity. we sat at a small
round table with piping mugs
of café con leche and you recited
a poem by Claribel Alegría that
said more than a thousand sermons
what needed to be known about
Central American identity and
hope. the smiles in the room told
us life will soon be tenderly woven
by the living.

I CAN'T BREATHE

yes, every least breath
draws life and church
people tell us about the
glory of a God who at
all times breathes. still,
we try to understand with
this shared divine breath
why we are choked like
Floyd to death. we hear it
said in church God took on
human flesh but no one you
see believes it was in colored
skin or to make Nazareth in
them. yes, we hear stories about
the redeeming cross outside the
city gate but white America comes
to set them one-by-one ablaze before
hanging us from trees. Lord, I hope
you don't mind when your church
gets to passing peace, joy, milk and
cookies around if we take the rage in
us and toss it like stones at the pulpits
bursting with unkept promises!

PRECIOUS NAME

I will not forget the tumbling
young Black men who flew in
the air to the music familiar to
us in a scorching country. they
were surrounded by a crowd of
New Yorkers and tourists from
far-away places for whom they
jumped, danced and spread their
arms with love. in the shade of
a building they leaped very high
with suffering blood and shouted
on occasion about private dreams
and more than a few memories as
the crowd smiled and clapped the
performance. I saw angels leaping
too from their hard brows and when
they lifted from the earth it was clear
this promised land was completely
theirs. the street was wrapped in the
identity of these young Black men
whose lives matter more than the
repulsive faith of the churches with
fenced front steps with signs that
read, "No Trespassing." I will not
forget today with lights in the theater
still out, a city emerging from illness

and these Black souls instructing the
public on a city sidewalk to say their
precious names.

LAZARO

I knew him from the
dirty metal factory by

the highway. workers
talked plain Spanish in

that place to interrupt
noise and eyes searched

around like they were in
a hurry to thread needles.

he worked trying to make
dreams while heaven quietly

watched. he stopped going
to church many years ago

convinced paradise was not
ever made for him by the

so-called Father who appears
to have vanished from his world

of pleas. I knew him before he
lost the tender sound of words,

when he talked about laughter
with family in a cooling wind

and stealing kisses from lovers.
I knew him in the factory where

the howl of other drifting souls
went out the front door, up the

street and poured into a pretty
Cathedral where God never listened

to them. I will never forget the day
he shared his disbelief and said in

death there would be no rest for
him. Jesus!

THE PORTRAIT

on the sidewalk
a gathered people
sips coffee from paper
cups underneath a cloudy
day around the corner from
St. John's Chrysostom Church
that rings morning bells with
priests on their knees inside
and the poor hurrying to
work. on the schoolyard
children gather for a day of
lessons on pavement where
flowers will not grow, while
mothers watch from a distance
imagining full lives for their
innocent young. from a window
across the street an old woman
sits in broken light banishing with
her smile despair.

CROSSING

standing on Second Avenue
with a light breeze sweeping
across the corners unconcerned
about the Spanish he speaks and
not having papers makes him
feel like a human being better
than legal. in this nearly 400
year old city, he is not eyed by
border guards and every block
has accents. he rides the subway
to work, chuckles on the station
platform with Salvadoran girls
new to the Bronx and listens to
an old Puerto Rican man who lost
a leg in a war that had nothing to
do with him speak against God.
he can hear the church bells from
the old Catholic Cathedral inviting
the neighborhood to prayer and
God to stay awake in the country
he calls home in which truth no
longer matters. on this side of
the border that he crossed on foot,
he is like the slaves who left Egypt,
crossed the parted sea and entered an
arid land to begin the march toward
a promised land.

A LESSON

some families get to see
the years run like fish in
a stream, children grow old,
and wounds heal up. some
write stories with an alphabet
to the public unknown, with
the tears of Whitman dripping
at night and witnesses that
keep diminishing. then there are
families never clear about what is
meant by a name, with pictures
kept in an old shoe box and kids
who live long enough to learn a
few lessons and wake up one day
all grown up.

DOPE

I never imagined it would
be a story different from one
of being led by the hand in
the barrio to Barbara's dope
den or walked down the street
by a junkie Puerto Rican poet,
listening to Héctor Lavoe sing
Aguanile in a Bronx funeral
home that has seen too many
kids off to eternity. I heard
people downtown complaining
about us, the spics threatening
their ways, stealing their daily
bread, speaking Spanish and
carrying on in a broken English
tongue. I always thought at the
end of the public-school year the
teachers would not invite us back
for another though it really mattered
little, since our lives were not in the
books, we had no Ricans for teachers,
no politicians in office, no cops on
the beat, no priests in church and no
one in the white world calling us human
beings. I never imagined surviving
four overdoses, a few stabbings, gun shots,

savage rumbles on the block or getting
plucked from generations of cruelty by
the simple gestures ironically of love
given to me by a white family, no less
frail, economically maimed and unwelcomed
in their world. I never imagined a visit from
the so-called Holy Ghost on the concrete sidewalks
of the South Bronx streets but it happened when
a preacher pulled a needle out of my adolescent
veins and led me to a slow new reading of the
gospel.

SIXTEEN

when a family took me in
at the age of sixteen I had
lots of experience in a world
that slayed my Spanish name
and never thought twice about
the South Bronx streets paved
by generations of Puerto Rican
blood. I confess the smells in
that new home were all novel to
me, macaroni and cheese, beef
goulash, meat and potatoes and
occasionally bluefish that always
came as a gift from the son-in-law
of a mafioso boss. I was lost for
too many years on the streets of
New York, Los Angeles, Newport
Beach, Santa Ana and Old San
Juan, almost forgot everything I
dreamed, hardly ever thought of
my near illiterate mother and father
who completed their nightmare in
the United States casting their boys
early into the world cause their labor
was not enough to make ends meet
and keep hungry kids. thinking of
the family that took me in, gave me

an English name, called me a son,
a big brother, taught me praise
Jesus songs and how to take those
breathless leaps into America
with my barrio dreams, leaves
me with a smile. in my thankful
years, I searched for my parents
found one in Ecuador, the other
in California. I broke the long
silence with awkward yet gentle
speech that erased the standard
lines about family, thanked them
for the gift of Spanish, the dignity
of culture and the short years of life
together. I embraced each of them,
shared the deep feeling of sadness
for not being raised by them into life,
and said the family grew across the
boundaries of difference and I want
you now to be at peace!

MAPES AVENUE

in 1967, on Mapes Avenue, Puerto
Rican kids heard the Beatles for the
first time who released Sgt. Pepper's
Lonely Hearts Club Band, the first
hand held calculator was invented by
Texas Instruments, troops increased
in Viet Nam, Muhammad Ali was
stripped of his world champion title
for refusing to be inducted into the US
Army, the Jewish clock repair man
lamented Israel's six-day war and
Manny went AWOL to escape combat
only to die from an overdose of dope in
a building stairwell smelling of piss.
there was marching in the streets for
civil rights, the end of war and every
lament ever imagined in the Bible, while
Pentecostal preachers were on corners
talking about how to escape the end
days. I became familiar with life beside
other broken English souls and with the
invisible Brown people living in the South
Bronx hated every 4th of July and rejection
by the American Dream.

THE HILL

I woke up in heaven that
morning hearing roosters
crowing the new day awake
and getting ready to make the
long hilly walk to the church
whose priest was familiar with
long sentences of hope. I did
not hear the report of gun fire
coming from the hills, went to
the kitchen window of the house
to look for boot prints left by
soldiers on the muddy road and
did not spot a single image. I
gave thanks for the grace of a
family walking indefatigably
ahead of the civil war, leaning
into each day with prayer and
scattering fear on the fields, the
mountains and village streets
visited by butterflies. perhaps,
that is why even when I write
the saddest lines my heart is
not blue for I have learned the
deeper meaning of love and it
fell into the bloodiest creases of
my heart.

UNDOCUMENTED

I can't recall after attending church
in about fifteen different countries
ever hearing the preachers ask about
God's border crossing papers. I would
have objected out loud in the middle of
the service at the suggestion of such an
obscene thought. about a month ago in
a tiny Texas town a man sitting next to
me in a pew put together by Mexican
carpenters suggested without a blush on
his white cheeks that God only speaks
English. I smiled rejecting to live in his
world where miracles do not take place
saying it seems to me your orderly house
is rather confused for God is a creator of
a whole lot of difference and you will not
find a more multilingual being. I went on
to say from the divine silence of the beginning
thousands of voices emerged and all that before
the first English word. it didn't matter to me
that this Texan likely didn't hear a word I said,
so I went on in public prayer to give thanks for a
heaven that watches over this earth from which
we all are made.

VOYAGE

life is a passage of here and
there, the dream of going back,
the place that never leaves one,
talk of everything and nothing,
a constant border crossing, a
time of severed faith, an endless
struggle in a losing country and
the light sought. life is the long
walk away from the curfew days
of a Spanish speaking village, the
mourning never answered by prayer,
the history of campesinos bled like
their ancestor slaves by dark-skinned
soldiers doing white deeds and finding
sleep with the unbearable desire to wake
up free. life is the scent of mangos
and coffee in the Lopez grocery store,
drifting wearily together with dreams,
children jumping rope in front of the
building with poor Jewish families still
in it, Puerto Rican flags on fire escapes
and new Salvadoran residents on the
block. life is taking the next step to the
promised land where villages are not
burned and tears are sweet.

SUMMER

the summer returns to the city
with the church bells ringing
that the kids on the block notice
by making the sign of the cross
over their hearts, while priests in
their hot Holy Mass in a near empty
church pray to find God leaning into
the spaces of the barrio. hunger is
left on the sidewalk in front of P.S.
20 that is serving Spanglish kids lunch
at the hands of sweet old white ladies
who take away their aches with sugary
words and often even a kiss. mothers
are not around in the summer days
off from school, they are busy with
the hard blows of life, wearied of
one-sided prayer and the constant
feeling of life cursed. the kids are
lifting themselves up today choosing
up sides for a stick ball game that will
last for more than an hour, then they
will settle a time of talk on the stoop
without a single word about the sadness
stored in their huge souls. in the summer,
they find ways to heal pain without any
of the old-time piety of churches where
Christ hangs above altars nailed to the
Cross.

BOARDS CREAK

when the subway rounds the
elevated track into Freeman
Station the abundant life God
promised might as well be a
train ride to Pelham Bay Park
and a delicate letter of apology
from the teachers, the cops and the
tickled white politicians who mangle
Spanish names. when South Bronx
born Willie Colon's music starts
to rise from the shadows in the old
apartment, the floorboards start to
creak and your mother croons Che
Che Cole from the only other room
in the place you know it is time to
see small explosions of light like
when the Nuns at St. John's church
walked you by hand the full length
of the Puerto Rican Day parade on
fifth avenue. when justice is done
to the wretched of the earth, the TV
evangelists shut up about their fabled
white Jesus and the courts let justice
roll down like waters for us then the
promises of heaven will have begun.

SERMONS

sermons are words to
a God who only listens,
never writes, gives pious
admirers a call, makes an
appearance in the worst of
times or parts the clouds in
the best of them. sermons
find many ways to sidestep
life, to overlook bruised Black
Brown, Red and Yellow skin,
to create a people that detests
hate, to say out loud beauty is
made in the colors of the earth,
seen in every protest, in miracles
for change, in prayers from the
languages of God's world and
the moans that leave all struggle
laden lips. sermons timidly speak
up and bore me with their images
that simply do not rise high enough
to heal broken hearts and let justice
scratch our skin.

THE RETREAT

the old woman had a private
book of prayer scribbled on
her heart. she looked at the
ticking clock with big hands
above the retreat house door
reflecting upon God on high in
the company of old widows with
lots to say from the weary dark
and beneath crying clouds. that
night, she was comforted by the
sweet bread that made her feel
like a vulnerable child enjoying
the delight of a simple thing. time
will never take away her cherished
hours, her patient waiting with the
ashes of a girl for Christ's loving
return and no longer thinking about
things lost. the retreat experienced
with aging friends could not deliver
more tenderness and hope than the
Lord's prayer recited by the watchers
of fragmented life.

FANTASY LAND

do you recall Yeats saying
some believe God leans a
hand from the sky to give
blessing yet no comfort ever
meets the expired bodies in
the grave. for the poet the
make-believe heaven offered
no escape from the daily grind
of graying life and the song of
the fairy world that always goes
unheard. we found this place of
thin hope on the corners of the
block, in the barrio shadows keeping
us a step ahead of brutalizing cops and
in our shuddering thoughts that are afraid
to carry us to a more favorable world.
perhaps, Yeats is right peace now and in
the unknown to come only wishes for the
things we imagine.

BLACKOUT

I thought it was a good idea to
wander the streets when the city
had a blackout yelling the world
is ending, to make my way to the
church down the block to borrow
a candle, to yell at the people who
kneeled on the sidewalk hunger is
finished in this great undoing of the
wounded earth and sit beneath the
old sky on a stoop finally to see a
night full of stars. I laughed with
lovers who shared mysterious kisses
on the building steps, at a Pentecostal
preacher rushing to find angry stones
with a message and the entire city that
was discovering the darkness finally of
the barrio. I confess it was a delicious
moment to feel grounded in our halfway
house lives, to experience the dark guzzle
up the lavish indifference of the makers
and shakers of a city keeping the working
class from realizing the justice of King
and their technicolor dreams.

SUNDAY

come Sunday a church with filled
pews, the one with standing only in
the aisles and the others with few
voices chanting prayers will know
heavenly fellowship just the same.
here where liquor stores are closed
come Sunday, people will say they
know where they came from and where
they are going the sacred day long when
God is felt among them. they will come
in clothes that slept all week in closets
to hear voices crying in the wilderness,
the echoes of flowing rivers, the singing
of young women who worked all week
as maids and the noise of children who
play games in the gospel space. come Sunday,
these people will carry their best dream book
under weary arms, in bags and verses that roll
off holy tongues. come Sunday, they will gather
to read a Bible that never changes its mind
about promises made for a world that likes to
walk in the wrong direction. come Sunday,
when services are done the sanctuaries will
hush and the time allotted us will once again
creep toward next week.

LOOK

I remember talking into the late
night with people objecting to a
world with deaf ears about the
distortions of faith and the unbridled
martyrdom of the poor paid for
by a country that needs death. in
the proper parishes people say that
was long ago and it is time now to
forget the ghosts that manufacture
pain, to move away from the bloody
stains of history keeping one awake
at night and settle into the ignorant
spaces of peace. I confess there are
too many of us who cannot keep from
crouching down behind the Cross of
a crucified rebel who always said more
than ever imagined about him, that cries
for us with nailed hands and feet and
casts his eyes upon us with the loving
fidelity of heaven. we must continue
to tell these altering stories that disturb
the memory of financiers, the orthodoxy
of the pious and the horrifying obscenity
of forgetfulness.

GOD WHO LOVES US

in the places visited by tropical
winds where you can even taste
the ocean salt in the air on the sides
of mountains the God who loves
us is troubled by the broken hearts
in the village homes, the children
who can't afford to attend school,
the families that survived civil war
that see youth flee and these churches
no longer speaking for the voiceless
and innocent. I can imagine God cries
for the poor in these places more than
for Jerusalem, knows our bitter history
better than the agonies of Christ hung
on a tree and must feel like a failure for
letting wickedness roam the world so
damn free. on the scales of divine love,
we have nothing left to weigh and not
a word to offer petitions to a so-called
God of love. the God who loves us has
kept quiet through hundreds of years of
bloodbaths and our weary tongues pray
so much God surely can't sleep.

STRANGER

I lost sight of you too many
years ago, and spent each day
trying to find you on bus rides,
trains from east to west, planes
flown to other countries, on the
corners of different cities and
churches celebrating Mass in
Spanish. I have carried you in
the pockets of cheap clothes in
a shanty town in Puerto Rico,
on my soaked cheeks on the
islands of the Caribbean, the
jungles of Central America and
Andean hills. I have searched
for you in dreams, the common
things of daily life and moments
of affection that come from those
met along the wandering ways of
life. you settled in me the day I
was born in a city hospital that
could not say your name and I
have entered these graying years
still carrying you dear mother
and yearning for the smell of rain
floating into the apartment from
the city and the noise of siblings
in the place we called home.

TRUTH

a cool breeze, a dog barking at
the window, Tito released from
detox, strangers smiling on the
sidewalk, abuelas not walking
alone, two boys on a stoop telling
the three little pigs sitting on a
fence story, laughter roaming the
block from the corner and curious
eyes blinking like butterflies from
the tenement windows. the people
today are too full of joy to roll their
eyes, to despair about a certain kind
of freedom overlooking the block, to
whisper about waiting for God with
skinny faith. today, the white haired
old men will play dominoes in front
of the bodega telling the truth about
the Brown history not taught to the
kids in school and the ordinary time
of the city will turn its head to listen
to them magically describe another
life. their stories will convince us to
look into each other's eyes and never
live a day with them closed.

PSALM 88

on 14th street by the East River
walk there are people living in
boxes and a few in donated tents
that are never mentioned by the
tourist boat that makes a loop of
Manhattan Island. dear creator
of the earth do something about
the blindness on the circle line,
let the people know you object
to the suffering of the poor, the
misery of the homeless and all
the yo-yo words said in dressed
up cushioned pew churches about
how change is gonna come. you
know, Hector and Carmen Julia
have lived beside that river for a
whole bunch of years and though
their faith like them has become
skinny with time they still light
candles for you. I do think it is
about time you gave them a sign
you are thankful! Incline your ear
to hear the words of the living among
the dead!

TAXI

the yellow cabs don't
go there from Times
Square. drivers have a
security system for rides
to the South Bronx, NO!
these hacks from other
wounded places of the
world wouldn't care if
you were the last person
on the earth. the human
is somewhere inside those
stone dead hearts so we
say on Simpson Street!

EXPECTING

it was clear Ana had little to
eat in her refrigerator and she
worried about the child in her
belly already named Sophia.
the neighborhood church bells
not made from melted bullets
like those in her little village
did little to satisfy the need for
a meal. the father had long ago
received his Notice to Appear
letter from *la migra* after a work
place raid that choked more life
out of him than the Rio Grande
he coughed up the night he had
to swim across the river. Sebastian
was deported to his old Cristobal
Colón world where the mariner
maimed, killed and started a fire
on a business trip that has not yet
ended. in Ana's world people have
too little and empty stomachs on
the cracked stoops regularly sing
in unison. Ana kneeled before
the altar in the apartment assuming
the penitent pose of an expecting
mother with no bread to eat, she

thanked La Virgen de la Paz for
allowing her to live in a city where
bombs were not loosening the old
tenement roofs and begged her to
send something to eat. there was a
knock on the door and Ana slowly
stood up to answer, looked through
the peep hole in the middle of the
door and noticed little Victor quietly
waiting for the door to swing open.
the little boy knew Ana and his mom
once worked together in the same place,
his mother got Ana a crib for the coming
baby and that morning he showed up
at her apartment with a bag of food
he purchased himself from the Perez
Bodega, after collecting tips from old
Jewish ladies by helping them carry
groceries home. Ana smiled at the
little boy whose kind gesture grabbed
hold of her heart with tenderness and
love. They sat together at the table
and ate buttered slices of bread and
gave thanks for another day!

TOSSED

deep in the alley
there is a place for
throw away kids by
the tenement trash
cans so the delinquents
who live there say. if you
ever got a postcard from
one of them you would
swear it came from a place
you never knew existed. these
tossed out kids were born in
the city, are new Americans
with Spanish names and they
have been pushed to the curb
by families that in America the
beautiful can't breathe. let me know
when you want to make your
way to the alley to talk with
them. then, after the visit,
from a place that makes you
feel like crossing the Jordan
tell others what you heard from
the mouth of God's own thrown
away kids.

STATIONS OF THE CROSS

he walked thousands of miles
doing the Stations of the Cross
for more years than memory ever
debated. he did not need to know
an ancient biblical language, to quote
scripture by heart, show a passport,
documents or prove his right to exist
in a world fixated on border check
points. he walked with healthy children,
sick friends, martyred priests, in the
heat of summer and the rainy season.
I suspect in the last five decades he
walked the distance to Jerusalem and
back more than a few times. sometimes,
he would stand in the little plaza of the
church where the processions all began
to stare at the Cross and I assumed he
heard it calling out to him and never let
heaven have the last word. I have walked
with him on many misty nights praying for
bread and wine to wash our Good Friday
world fully clean. often, I asked is God
listening to us? Does God really need to
forgive those living in places intoxicated
with sorrow? I will keep walking with him,
circling the Good Book and hope to find an
end to the thick silence.

THE BARRIO

the barrio is with us
in the places they tell
us to get out, in hellish
memories of what was
left, in unemployment
lines, kids at school not
speaking Spanish, on the
curb drinking wine, the
rooftop shooting dope,
in the prison gang and
every time Brown kids
for no reason get hauled
off to jail. the barrio is
with us in the miscarried
prayers that never reached
heaven, the broken English
kids without parents and in
all the ways we endure life
in a world that is still in love
with confederate flags, statues
and the colored dead. the barrio
is with us in the faces of despised
human beings and in the exquisite
miracles unseen.

YOU LIVED!

the last time I saw you
breathing air on Walton
Avenue the cops were
chasing Papo down the
street. I looked around
for a place to take cover
in case the shots started
to ring holding a brand
new copy of Bonhoeffer's
The Cost of Discipleship
that caused me to offer up
a brief prayer like I never
learned in seminary requesting
a little more life to finish the
martyred theologians' book
and enjoy one more dinner with
you at the Cuchifrito restaurant
on the formerly white Grand
Concourse. I always praised the
way you habitually made it out of
tough situations alive and I agreed
with the required text I happened
to be clutching that Sunday that
you were as entitled to grace as
anyone in church and certainly
far more than the money creed

preachers.   when I buried you
a few months later, it was clear
America cut out your tongue in
the name of uncommitted crimes
as Adorno would say.

THE CARRIERS

on old West Farms Road
the Puerto Rican girls were
skipping rope on the sidewalk,
a group of boys were hitting a
Spaulding ball against a wall
with their hands, old men were
playing dominoes and the block
was shaking with laughter. the
look on every face disclosed it
was a happy day and a fine time
to hear the certain Spanish words
remembered yet hardly spoken.
today, smiles spread across the
Brown faces like fire bouncing
on a field of dry grass and the
deepest hope of the neighborhood
came out to play. no one cared
to debate that we were home right
here in this Spanglish piece of the
city that carries our whole story
like the martyred King carried
dreams to the regal marble pose
of Lincoln.

GRAY YEARS

we have imagined scribbles
on a map that tell stories too
well known by greying hair
of dreamy places, childhood
with ethical innocence, life
in the shadows of Northern
cities, the feeling that youth
was too quickly done and
delicious moments carried
together by love. still, we
smile for the memories have
not retired to the places where
people go to play bridge, which
is a good thing for we don't know
the game and I suspect for the
sake of our Latin American souls
never will. often, we sit quietly
now talking with just a look of
the eye and I always see the same
face beaming with the wind blowing
your hair and ready for the deepest
joys to emerge from recollections or
the yet to come.

AWAKE

the morning belongs to
me lovelier than it will
last, filling the spaces
of memory, unleashed
like a child running for
the first time, delighted
by singing birds, younger
than butterflies resting on
flowers and so full of the
eternal beauties of life. I
want to remember it on
days its greatest meaning
will be clearest to me.

THE POMPOUS

in the early evening you can
see the outline of the Palisades
beside the Hudson River from
a little park on Morningside
Heights within a few blocks
of the school that is home to
theologians who spend time
instructing another generation
of ministers of grace. today, it
was warm enough for a walk on
the banks of the river and ponder
the truths offered in classrooms
you sometimes feel tremble when
they spread accidentally into the
wrong side of the world known too
well by people in the barrio. the
sweet theologians have wandered
too long in Plato's cave to consider
the tortures of the poor that condemn
their near mute God. they are well
trained to spin beautiful tales that
for the most part never call nailing
a human being to a tree a plain and
simple lynching. when the world is
so dark that it questions the morality of
God, I have heard them declare blessed
are the meek and those who wait on
the Lord. Shit! ¡No joda!

BELOW

on Saturday night he walked
to the corner of Saint Mark's
Place with a Bible under his
arm that spoke Spanish and
English. he planned to share
with the neighborhood what
he read about the God who
answered his questions. it did
not occur to him that evening
that others on the Lower East
Side had questions too long
for his Lord to hear and they
never needed and distasted the
command to love others. he was
on the corner for several hours
shouting words that never let
his heart kneel low enough to
consider that a sledge hammer
cannot pound any truth into a
single troubled soul and like
Emily said it argued him pretty
narrow. Tito happened to be on
his way across town when the
corner preacher declared from his
reading no doubt God is merciful
and Tito cracked up thinking that
from the perspective of the gallows
hanging the truth in the barrio too
damn unjust.

THE GARDEN

on 3rd Street there is a garden
growing vegetables and flowers
on a lot that housed in a brick
tenement people from Southern
Europe with lives thinned across
the lands they called home before
landing on Ellis Island. they were
no less rejected and far too many
citizens believed unworthy wretched
refuse from shores across the great
pond and no different from the spics
with a garden on the Lower East side,
now. I have not seen a more beautiful
urban garden than the one on this street,
full of piece-work talked to in Spanglish
every morning, teeming with tiny colorful
flowers, full of row after row of beans,
corn, peas and lettuce that speak their own
language of justice for everyone who walks
by to see. I have sat in the garden beneath
full moons inhaling the sweet fragrance of
flowers, talking with the urban farmers who
offered café Bustelo with exuberant island
hospitality and to bring night out of darkness
laughing outrageously loud at the very idea
of a secret garden. no, this exquisite garden
will inherit the earth!

ADAM PURPLE

I saw an old man dressed
in tie dye purple clothes
on a bicycle on the horse
and buggy path in Central
Park. he was collecting
manure for his concentric
garden on the Lower East
Side where everyone called
him Adam Purple. little did
I know when I looked into
that bearded Missourian face
the old man was on a mission
to build a new Garden of Eden
in the East Village and thought
long before it was fashionable
of the importance of protecting
the earth. Adam was a white
man with a utopian vision of
life and the Puerto Rican kids
spent time playing among his
meticulously planted 15,000
square foot garden of flowering
shrubs, fruit trees and plants in
concentric circles that yielded
a yin-yang symbol visible from
rooftops. Adam Purple was

one of fifty subjects in Harvey
Wang's New York photography
book and a technicolor human
being in every imaginable way.
nothing put smiles on our faces
more than seeing this skinny, slightly
hunched, long white bearded and
wrinkled man squatting an abandoned
building like the poor and building his
Garden of Eden. sadly, in 1986, the city
bulldozed Adam's Garden to make way
for housing and flowers in it closed one
last time in the stinking wind.

THE JOURNEY

I rolled across the country
in a Gran Torino at a very
tender pre-teen age staring
out the passenger window
searching for mystic signs
on the road that I read about
in books in a reading room
of the New York City library
with lions that guarded the front
door. on the ride hope was with
me though it was small and near
drowned more than a few times
on the way to LA. I was just old
enough then to clean drool from
my own shirt and question the
messes of home. I rolled the car
window down to scream in Spanish
expecting words to be carried all
the way back to the Bronx and with
the hippie giving me the lift I talked
about what was left in the barrio until
he learned more than a few Spanglish
words. I still had the rosary given to
me at first communion a couple of
years earlier, touched it from time to
time imagining potent magic for the

trip and thought that the callous heart
in the home that kicked me to the curb
needed hanging on the alley clotheslines
to dry. while waiting on the long ride
to get to the West Coast my pulsating
heart already imagined a new existence
back in school. you can imagine when
I finally got to the city of Angels the
word hope turned out not to be an English
term I owned.

FAR

he lived in a furnished room
with cheap things to match
his wages. he believed in a
savior long dead that only a
hand full of followers saw in
the Middle East many years
ago. at night, he held long
talks with God about getting
too old to be poor, not keeping
track of his daughter and what
the world will be when he is
gone. will the dogs still bark
in the alleys? will Miguelito
sit on the stoop on Saturday night
to play his conga? will Margarita
dance on the corner to the salsa
blaring from the Pizza shop with
fancy speakers? will the pigeons
still land on Shorty's fire escape
to do each other's plumage while
the kids play stickball in the middle
of the street? will the priest say
Mass in his name and the widows
light candles for his soul? his furnished
room was a quiet hiding place where
he supposed a distant God would find
him soon.

HISTORY

we have been making history
for centuries on this land but
I bet you can't name the first
Latinx farmer, soldier, pilot,
doctor, lawyer, teacher, politician,
scientist astronaut, judge, baseball,
basketball, football or tennis player.
I bet you never read a word about
us in the Reader's Digest and
white contract historians have a
fondness for leaving us out
of their narrative and misspelling
our names. you may believe the
pious white lies that say we all
crossed the border just yesterday
but next time you see pictures
of the Texas Rangers lynching
young Brown men remember
this land has a history that says
Sylvia Mendez just like Ruby
Bridges integrated schools in
the name of equality.

NUYORICAN CAFÉ

after eleven, when the door opened
to the café words came through it
from a slam poet at the mic and I
traveled through them into the aging
Nuyorican Eden. thousands of nights
in the barrio pushed their way out of
her mouth and the audience laughed
and cried at the same time. the Lower
East Side is a long way from Harlem
but quietly in this café for nearly five
decades the Nuyorican Renaissance
in spoken word has been underway and
its temporality is enshrined by a long
list of names in print. when I sit here
with the weary who wonder what's left
to dream until the dawn and the last
poet turns off the mic that leaves the
room noisy with silence, I thank the
laughing God who let us move about
with our Spanglish wounds without
feeling lonely in darkness. I will come
back again to listen to bittersweet words
shared by brothers and sisters that enter
me and stick to the knot in my throat
until I cough them back into the big old
world.

AMERICA

the beautiful things are fleshed
with thoughts beneath the moon
and the caressing air that belongs
to us. the federal politicians with
sweet rot apples on their desks can
not take them away no matter how
many ways in their private clubs they
come up with conduct to beat dark people
to their knees. the fierce affirmation of
life stands up to sing on the corners of
the city about life, irrepressible light and
ideals far from the mumbo jumbo of white
supremacists' fantasies of moral and ethnic
superiority. we are the ones who will carry
the nation, the exiles, the aliens, freed slaves,
first nations, and the men, women and children
with broken grammar tongues proposing a
fresh new world.

THE MARKET

on the Lower East Side
with a face lifted Second
Avenue the peddlers are
rummaging the garbage
cans for stuff to sell in the
little park. a couple of them
have shopping carts that look like
they date back to the pushcart days
of the Essex Street market that
is now at home on a new corner
selling specialty foods for deep
pocket people. the neighborhood
has changed, no sleeping on the
pavement, no panhandling, no
public drinking, spitting, crying
or talk about the poor and broken
English stories that will make the
laughter in the condos stop. the
beggars who have faces like lighted
candles are nonetheless impossible
to miss.

THE FALL

some nights the tempest in my
heart must speak old words that
are new by the time they reach the
open air. there are weeks too that
go by with a hunger to be fed and
an insatiable thirst quenched by a God
that speaks. other times I want to sit
and listen to the world from a city stoop
until exhaustion and the hunched back
pigeons perch on the fire escapes to caste
mysterious gazes over me. other times I
want to tell the priests up the street to learn
to be Angelic by talking with Rosa the prostitute,
Hank the Midnight Express wino, Rudy the
junkie, Ana the teen mother, Nana the holocaust
survivor and every child living the fall. tonight,
though I want you to point me in the direction
of the river Jordan or at least the path that starts
the journey toward the place where dark flesh and
fragile bones walk on water.

THE SUBWAY

on the subway the man
with a blue sport coat is
reading The New York Post
glancing up to get a look
at people now and again. a
young woman seated next
to me looks over my shoulder
to see I am reading Merton's
Seven Story Mountain and
little did she know I was then
wondering how many stories
were in mine. we looked into
each other's eyes for a moment
then returned to different affairs
on the subway ride downtown.
the guy reading the Post flipped
excitedly to the sports section and
popped a piece of candy in his perfect
teeth mouth. from time to time, I looked
up to see the faces of those around me
in the glass windows of the subway car
aware that passengers would eventually
come to their station and pop out of
train doors like a magician's pigeon
from a top hat.

COCONUT ICES

in the summer, he repaints the
coquito pushcart, counts the bags of

sugar and coconuts for making
fine coconut ice treats and when

the wells are ready he makes it
to the main street walking past the

buildings with apartments filled
with Spanish names. walking

his cart he yells in the direction of
the children looking out of windows

coquito and they shoot their voices
back at him. he goes past the spot

where Moisés took his last breath and
the tenement behind the stain he left

on the sidewalk was condemned by
the city shaking his old head. in a tiny

side compartment he placed on the cart
the man hides a handful of letters that

have walked for the last eight summers,
were never mailed but packaged with love

for a wife and a couple of kids remembered
by the hour and not seen in all the years

of life on this side of the border. again,
he yells coquito and the eyes on the

street are drawn immediately to the
words painted in red on the side of

the cart: *Delicioso Coco Helado.*

WATER

I bet you never thought water
could cry. on sleepless nights
in cold winter we can hear it on
the other side of the window
dripping from the roof and the
faucet in the bathroom where roaches
scatter when lights are turned on.
I swear those six leg creatures in
the apartments look like they object
to the sobbing. yesterday, the hall
leading to the front door was drenched
given the kitchen where the hungry sit
to stare at each other could not keep
from spilling tears. some nights, I have
walked the apartment with a candle in hand
searching the darkness for the crying to
join the enigmatic waterworks. on these
search nights, I often thought perhaps the
water-carriers will show up to pick up the
young and put an end to the sobbing.

THE PEASANT

does the campesino
who spends day after
day picking coffee
sipped thousands of
miles away have a
name for God? do
manicured priests
and preachers ever
talk of these workers
lives? do scholars
still write books about
peasants who whisper
to each other about the
land that was once
their very own? do
you know this man
works hard and his
kids living across
the border scribble
broken English curses
on the sidewalk with
colorful chalk to let
you deeply see into
hurt souls.

THE RETURN

one day they will return
with slow feet, a little less
occupied with dreams and
searching what remains
despite no longer working
old prayers. one day they
will return looking for the
places where they kept the
candles lit, faces of friends
more aged and breathing the
air of these Mesoamerican
mountains like they never
left. one day they will return
with stories of those who faced
detention, workplace raids,
children forgetting Spanish
and time moving slowly in the
white country with a heart of
stone. on that day, the villages
in this tiny country will kneel
like they were never flattened.

THE NAME

we don't need to see your
monuments, hear stories of
your martyred heroes, recall
out loud the history of your
Exodus from religious strife
across the pond and confess
your version of the covenant
with God.   the blood stained
land knows the martyrs we all
weep, the border is a monument
we named and the exile lived by
those of us forced to leave other
lives and loves on distance shores
for the new Babylonian lament that
raises our kids. we can't stand to
hear any more stories of a white
Jesus who is jubilant about the
progress your world has made
on the suffering and death of
darker human beings. we sing
to a lynched refugee, a homeless
human being, a bastard child who
ended life on a tree lanced by a
spear made from the bright ideas
of an empire that hardened into
your English speaking world.

CATECHISM

once a week they let us
out of school to sharpen
a few beliefs with priests
offering what they called
religious instruction. the
best part was getting out
of school an hour early,
playing kick the can all
the way to the old church
and preparing questions
with lots of imagination
to trip the theologians.
Shorty had already seen
the inside of a jail cell on
Rikers Island, Tito saw
his brother shot, Papo's
little sister died of an OD
from El Viejo's dope and
I witnessed my mother
get beat up by a husband
and more than a single
boyfriend. on religious
instruction day the fancy
office in the church would
never experience the wind
blowing in slanted sunlight

the way it had become familiar
to us. we were getting ready
in the eyes of the church
for first communion in
which God ingested would
be no less invisible than
Manolo who disappeared
at the age of thirteen from
the block. I can still hear
the long prayers exhaled
in Father Rossi's office
and remember each day
at the cemetery when we
buried catechism class
chums.

VAYA

I hear the salsa band playing
from an improvised stage down
by Avenue C. you can see on
the musicians faces that tonight
they want to get it all said, to
knock out the tropical rhythms
that will stir the world to some
kind of utopia like the one first
dreamed in the village of Lares
and tease the edges of time until
it favors the slum. I see Brown
hands banging out the songs of
a Puerto Rican soul on the congas,
another dancing on keyboards like
tomorrow was the end of the world
and only musical fools have time for
one more raggedy night. I hear the
singer on stage conquering the room
with her voice, using sweet tropical
harmonies to disentangle our souls,
binding our hearts and tears when I
I scream, Vaya!!

DAYS LEFT

every morning love awakes
and time is lost to the world.
without knowing what to call
this life without papers on the
north side of the border, we
walk around apartments scoring
another day off the calendar on
the wall. the loneliness is never
chased away by submersion in
books, the Spanish evening news,
long city walks or sobs drowned in
the park with spirited drinks. it stays
with us in the overcrowded tenement,
the secret places where we gather and
in the labor halls. every morning the
cooing of the mourning doves bear your
name translated into stories recalled in
a different world and those who listen to
what is said know something full of grace
will one day answer.

MALT LIQUOR

in those days in the Bronx
we sat on the stoop drinking
Colt 45 and with nothing more
than words walked past the fancy
stores downtown. we imagined
them selling fashionable clothes,
getting lost in their carefully laid
out labyrinth of display halls and
yelling before exiting que viva
Puerto Rico! we could hear the
murmurs from the corner, the
rapid fire bitter tongues born in
foreign countries, the denial felt
for a God who promises all will
be well and the comforting voices
of the stumbling old grandmothers
who loved us. after a few sips, we
imagined climbing the bell tower
of the local Catholic church where
we were all baptized just to look
over the block and yell at priests
who kneel without shame on these
streets so far from God. in those days
we sipped beer, listened to Symphony
Sid's salsa radio show and were very
convinced that hunger and indigence
were the only sure things resurrected
on the block.

THE HOMILY

I listened
to words
kindly speak
of grace
and
push sadness
to the
marshes of
a distant
shore.
in the dim
light of
a church
you could hear
laughter,
sobbing
and
restless kids
celebrating the
life
of a woman
who could
not stay
and
now rests
in the loving
arms of
the God

that claimed
her.
we gathered
aware
that silence
is not dark,
forever is a
forested land
of grace
and
death
has
no sting.

SCENT

the scent of a summer morning
rushes into you visible like the
half-moon leaving for the rest
of the day. the aroma causes
certain memories to arise like
secrets with the fragrance of
flowers that are full of the things
you have carried for years that
waited for you. nature invades
your sight like it was in the very
beginning and you admit with
every dirty tear and inhalations
of air that you are cut from the
same stuff of the earth. perhaps,
today you will kiss the doorless
wind in every direction, put your
heart in the world and live more
fully than ever.

WASHINGTON SQUARE

the wind blows water
from the fountain at the
center of the park into
the curious faces. on the
Southwest corner of the
square travelers' who walk
with weighted dreams stop
to play a round of chess. the
children on the playground
wear faces that make many
pedestrians think perhaps this
is a dream. trees looking older
than the Greenwich Village are
silent, dogs in every color, size
and shape bark, a man lifts a
baby into the air who kisses the
emptiness, faint stars begin to
spread their light and the park
crowd is plunged into an odd
awakening faith. slanted wood
benches in this woke place give
rest to hearts that are eager and
full of longing though none of
us can clearly say why.

DELTA STRAIN

it's too late to wail
over the parting that

is your fault, the politics
against the better sense

in life or the virus in the
lungs that kill. it's too

late to look away from the
poor, the middle class and

mighty ones who are never
shunned in shanty towns,

modest homes or palaces
alike of the mighty Delta on

its graveyard marches. it's too
late to deny the disease that

plows innocent flesh and blood
until no matter the color of the

human being it cannot deliver a
single breath. it's too late to

point fingers except at lovers
of misery, right-wing foolery

and the brutal ignorance that
makes us sick. it's not too late

to follow drops of hope made
by tears in the suffocating air of

a frightened, panicked and divided
nation.

OTHERS

they practiced religion
when the wind swept the

leaves of palm trees and
in the hard times of broken

down tenements clinging
to the hope for answered

prayer. they worked hard
in the fields, the factories,

restaurants, office buildings,
churches, with other peoples

kids waiting for any prophet
to whisper objections. once

a week they went like sinners
to the altar with bodies fasting

without choice expecting to
receive assurance of salvation

while others in fancy clothes
dined and decided how they

would die. they picked up
stones to throw at the Citibank

building, the mayor's riverside
home and the subsidiaries of

death supported with billions
in tax exemptions that exhaust

the poor into premature screaming
graves. they left for the world of

muted Saints and the place Christ
never appeared leaving behind kids

with leaded blood and accused of
everything wrong in America.

THE CAB DRIVER

the taxi driver came to NYC
from Bombay after wrestling
demons in Singapore for a few

long years. in the early hours
of the morning when business
slowed he imagined life again

knowing what he knows and
collected beautiful images on
the drive down Fifth Avenue

while fingering a charm in his
shirt pocket. I climbed into his
world to get to the East Village

swiftly, a wino with a sign that
read collecting funds for wine
research taped on his window at

14th Street but he didn't get a
cent. the driver tells me the city
was a ghost town for months in

the pandemic, people were carried
out of buildings dead, bodies were
stored in refrigerated trailers, the

city was stuck midway to nowhere
and masks hid frightened faces. the
mythology of a city of incurable joy

seemed never truer to the taxi driver
than before the time of illness and
endless grieving. I listened to him

say the vaccine has changed the feel
of the city and said amen when he
suggested a memorial needed to be

raised with the names of the innocent
dead so the blood in our veins never
runs cold and the life together that was

lost can be honorably mourned.

SNOW WHITE

when I was a child my first
experience of a white world

was the story shown on a black
and white TV of Snow White

and the Seven dwarfs. I
could not forget the faces of

the magical little men and
looked for them in alleys,

rooftops and the long walks
to school. I looked for them

everywhere on the block, at
Orchard Beach and even swore

laying eyes on the very innocent
Snow White sitting on a towel with

blue eyes at Section One by the sea.
the story says no beauty could surpass

the fair girl and I dared to disagree for
Margarita with her long Black hair,

nourishing dark eyes and tamarind
skin was more beautiful than a mirror

would ever admit. once upon a time
remained the best way to hear a story

start and though I never found the little
puzzled men or Snow White anywhere

on the block there were people enough
in Spanglish town to tell different tales

about evil queens, little wise men, days
of adversity and people never soiled by

the appetite of love and alive in simple
little things.

PREACH

I could almost see stitched
on the altar cloth the lofty
thoughts rich with denials
about the barrio. they jumped
at me just like the scandalous
meditations that go out of their
way to escape the poor. I wait
hoping to hear God made a world
where truth is glimpsed on lucky
days despite the veils but the preacher
does not hint it and nothing is said
of the flaws of creation and the
nation presumed a city set on a
hill. does your God know about
the tragedies mounting up in the
barrio like images in a very ugly
looking-glass? I must confess
heaven is a great distance from
earth though the preacher says
it is an inch removed!

AFTER SCHOOL

yesterday, I picked my daughter
up at school and she climbed into
the car and asked me to drive her
to the Hong Kong Market for she
had a craving for squid and other
snacks to satisfy her intercultural
palate. without knowing, I followed
her up and down the aisles with shelves
of items labeled without English and
it was like following the child in a cave
of water. she sat on the drive home glad
with squid in the back seat of the car
laughing in tongues and delighting me
with simple mystery. then, she reminded
me of the French bulldog she glimpsed by
a fountain in Washington Square Park that
was breathing dreams. at the stop light, she
showed me a picture of one and pleaded with
me to acquire the pup. when I saw the $4000
cost it occurred to me in that moment of fatherly
bonding to smile and say, "honey, it's a beautiful
pup but for the price I prefer to wait to find one
that can read, write and talk, so let's keep looking."
she sighed, "Daaaad" then displayed an endearing
smile that I caught in the rearview mirror!

RALLY

today, I saw malevolent
stones dangled from trees
and waiting to be picked
by vile hands to again make
Herod great. you may have
heard it reported in the evening
news unless the volume on
your devises were turned down
and you pretended to be like
the deaf young man who rides
the subway carrying a cup for
change. I cannot begin to tell
you how the latest other guy
rally is a knife in the heart and
a gathering of imbeciles who
are still trying to figure out how
to bury Black, Brown, Yellow
and Red humanity alive. as a
poet if I could write God into
this scene waters everywhere
would part and Rahab would
sing to America in Spanish
like Rosita the Simpson Street
hooker about what it means
to live in a history full of too
much rot.

BURNING BUSH

I have not seen a burning bush of
fire on the sidewalks of the city. if
I happened to see one it would speak
in the loveliest broken English to coax
me to listen. I would invite the voice in
the flame on the tumbling lower east
side to tell a few more stories only less
embellished by deceit. I would ask the
divine disclosure to take me to a place
by the river to find stones that never
miss when thrown from undocumented
shores. I would of course ask about all
the letters sent for blessings returned to
their senders and complain a little about
how expertly the refrigerators were left
empty, the people unemployed, children
dropping out school, youth locked up in
jails, fields harvested for the rich, factories
worked by the poor, white kids raised by
Latina maids, cops beating Spanglish town
to death and cries never heard in the pretty
white-faced church. I suppose we will have
to wait a little longer and pray the fire in the
bush still burns or find a savior in the ordinary
human beings stooped down by work and the
immeasurable curses in God's own broken
world.

THE TOUR

I heard you are going on
the Hip Hop tour of the
South Bronx to look at
the Mural of Big Pun and
listen simply to sidewalks
whisper about its frail origin
with Black and Puerto Rican
tongues. I suspect you will
hear sounds carrying stories
from the corners, the fainting
lives of junkies and the pistol
wiped people. if you had known
these streets with phone booths
on each block, found the scraps
of letters never mailed from the
apartments and listened to kids
in the storefront church raping
prayers with their waiting room
patois, perhaps you would have
called the federal department of
promises to say it's time to fling
the swamp things down the sewer,
put the church up against wall
for not doing a damn thing and
like a kneeling penitent request
the disdained be loved.

AGING

each year I age a little more
like an old newspaper, a hymn
hardly sung or a flower in a vase
still colorful and bright in outlived
time. I talked with a friend who
already settled on the senior shore
to watch a river flowing gray while
steadying his legs with the help of
a stylish cane. he lamented for a
good long time about the problems
that come with aging though his eyes
disclosed a child still craving for the
happiness life offers without waving
goodbye. I sat with him staring at the
dark water of the East River aware of
the threat he felt in the senior condition
and observing the deep note of existence
on the field beside us where children ran
a game of football. I put my arms around
him to say we are like children given a
bunch of quarters for the arcade just to
pleasure the soul and not even treasonous
sleep aging us at night will cause the quiet
and constant light to drift away.

SINGLE STRING

he was on the corner
late last night playing
for a small crowd around
him on a single string
guitar. directly above
his head Golgotha was
shining through a street
light that made him for a
moment the center of
salvation. he cradled the
unusual instrument while
the listeners fell over their
smiles when notes from the
single chord reached an ear
and gathered questions in
their minds. it was quite easy
to find music passing from
the homeless musician into
us without need of explanation
or fancy words. I listened calling it
the music we need on that East
Village corner where life yawns
when questions explode.

SCHOOL

I counted the new cars
parked beside the school

that belonged to teachers
who never lived in a city

slum. today, when snow
turned the sidewalks white

I saw the math teacher's
red Camaro stationed in

the cold wind with seats
still warm from the long

drive to the Bronx. I saw
lights on in classrooms

from Arthur Avenue that
made me think of church

and outstretched hands
that belonged to people

who just want to live. I
entered the school with

too many teachers who
disapproved of Black and

Brown kids with braided
hair and their world beneath

the cackling better off. I sat
at my wooden desk and read

lines scribbled on it that offered
a prayer not read by clear eyes

and never heard by a ready-made
God and so I wrote one too without

saying a thing to the fugitive from
heaven giving a lesson at the

front of the room.

DANTE FESTIVAL

in the simplicity of vernacular
speech, the mother tongue of
masses, a displaced Italian poet
who roamed the murky circles
of hell scattered in it the words
of common tongues. the world
never regretted the denunciation
of Babel the poet described as the
sighs and weeping of diverse speech
and the punishment of God for sheer
ignorance. in a world of different
tongues, the Dante Alighieri gives us sweet
verbal hybridity, the blending of
other voices and the subversive power
of spaces opened to the polyphony
of words where heaven spreads itself
across the sky to hint of more hopeful
times. the Tuscan poet has walked
with me carrying copies of work by
Langston Hughes in the pocket of
my trousers always steering me to
the enduring truth that confirms my
Spanglish belongs in time and space
forever.

HOLY LAND

each year with life a little
more spent, the heart I am

told grows a little older and
fonder of dazzling nights in

the company of stars and the
simplicity of solitude. surely,

in the centerless world we wait
for the slow movements of an

absolute sign, a humble glimpse
of revelation or at last the second

coming. in this world full of
with tears I find myself slouching

toward the Holy Land that for me
is across the Mexican border and

it is there that the living face of
God comes wandering from the

hills and out of the corn fields
calling out my name. in that land

more sacred than Jerusalem, I will
sit until life is spent listening to the

everlasting voices of my people of
corn who are older than the Holy

book found in church.

IGNORANCE

unhappy are those who
cannot see with scientific
eyes and find themselves
content with conspiracy
and lies. they burn good
books, deny any truth and
claim the earth is flat. they
try to forget their intubated
kin and friends and fill their
days with ignorance in an
age of illness that demands
reasonableness from speech.
I hear them say the Lord is
their shepherd but soon they
shall want to exhale longer
thoughts in the places they live.
with fat words they have made
the pandemic little, laughed at
a world in illness and screamed
stupidity like it was a brilliant
prize. can it be too late to bring
the country back to healing? surely,
whispers are useless to anyone in
an age of sickness!

SHINE, MISTER

with this money earned shining
shoes I will buy a baseball glove,
open a savings account with a
dollar in the bank, buy a single
flower for Mami and a slice of
dreams dripping from cotton
ball clouds. I will buy a fare
for a subway ride downtown
and see the numerous faces walking
around the Central Park Lake.
I will sit the afternoon in the Great
Meadow confessing the earth is
round and cursing in Spanglish
the mariners, mercenaries and
conquistadores that bleed us into
life centuries ago though we did
already belong to the earth. who
knows, I may save a buck to buy
what I must understand after 500
years!

LABOR DAY

when the wells dried of water,
the coffee fields went bloody

red and the rivers darkened with
bodies they ran for the fields of

English speaking farmers to fill
harvest wagons, to churches that

hardly called la migra and to the
crooked steel of cities where they

joined other laborers with agonized
flesh. through many years, they

have labored for America to eat in
fields, slaughterhouses, countless

kitchens and homes. in cages of
helpless sleep the broken English

maids just weep before a new day
begins full of cooking meals, washing

floors, ironing clothes and tending
to the needs of innocent little white

kids. Labor Day is just another fever
upon these shores, Esperanza rounded

up in a work place raid with the president
on a coast-to-coast television hook-up

thanking workers, Jesus hiding in the
remains of a harvested cornfield and

dark fleshed new Americans growing
up in a tempestuous nation that will

pluck out their eyes before they ever
get a chance to see the prize. Labor

Day was not invented for the tired
hands of undocumented human beings

who daily pray Lord have
pity on us.

TELEVISION

America loves to collect odd things
from the looks of what is playing on

TV. serial killers seem always to be
romanticized, men are glorified by

their acts of violence, women are
made into Delilah, sexually objectified

and banally displayed in countless
reality shows. sitcoms are peppered

across the many channels in half hour
segments and classic reruns of an old

white man ranting from his favorite
chair in a Queens living room still

can make you on occasion care. then
there are the news shows spinning tales

for the public, sharing images that show
Black, White, Red, Yellow and Brown

walking very different fine lines, covering
social issues with lies, half-truths and a

whole lot of carefully composed escape
from the agonized lives in the ghetto and

the world sanctimoniously stomped by
American empire. just once I would like

to see on that TV screen images of ICE
being chased by cross carrying citizens,

widows with Rosaries screaming their names,
Dreamers with placards painted with perfect

English words telling us they live and
humanity in its luxurious diversity all

around them on the Lower East Side.

BREAD

he carried home in a
backpack given to him
in the Catholic thrift shop
on Hoe Avenue. he walked
streets in the Bronx and on
Manhattan island collecting
bottles and cans from litter
baskets and reciting poetry on
the corners with an empty
cup in front of him. he spoke
truth about a hollow world,
made up metaphors of palm
trees reaching for the sky to
shade giants more than ten feet
tall and the Pentecostal preachers
who could not heal winos with
manicured hands. once a month,
he pulled the wrinkled leather belt
around his waist a little tighter and
told himself no matter how many
times he reads the words in the tiny
Bible given to him at the shelter it
would not turn into bread.

ADAGIO

we gathered on the corner
sitting on old wood crates to

listen to Miguel play congas
and collect words we refined

into songs about home troubled
hearts. buses rolled down the

street, car horns beeped a block
away, kids yelled in a game of

stick ball they played in the middle
of the street and all this noise was

turned into fresh beats by Mike
the conguero. we listened to his

drumming hands that lifted sadness,
made us laugh and even imagine

nightingales that not one of us had
ever seen in real life singing loud

and near. we gathered at the same
spot where last night's wind rattled

tenement windows and whispered
that is an adagio into our ears and

told us there is more to come. who
would have thought you could sway

your hips ever so slowly just listening
to a breeze.

SHOES

every couple of years I
recall getting a new pair

of shoes that my mother
took to the repair shop to

have taps put on the toes
and heals to make them

last. my feet slipped into
them like they were a soft

bed, talked to them all day
while I sat in school trying

to pay attention to lessons
that upset my soul with

irrelevance and I wore them
even when they got holes

in the soles that I fixed up
by slipping cardboard inside

of them. I recall mother buying
them a little big so I would grow

into the things and I escorted those
shoes to P.S. 66, St. John's church

and down Manhattan streets like
somewhere on them eternal truths

would rush us. I remember one day
seeing people exiting the Fifth Avenue

Cathedral where eulogies were said
for Robert F. Kennedy who did not

follow easy paths and when I walked
pass the front entrance I made the sign

of the cross and wrapped my childish soul
in the Spanish words of simple prayers that

let me wander with holes in my shoes
and confess the day long the only way

to live is to dream in troubled times.

DREAM, AGAIN

we have all touched time
and learned to tell stories
with depth for years to
come. the seasons have
spread out from tropical
shores, rain forests, thin
air mountains, widening
deserts and in the world
where we have learned
English and watched kids
forget the dear language
that trills r's. the history
books have little memory
of us, their authors never
weep with shame. today,
we who have bled, suffered
and mourned on this boasted
land of liberty called America
lift every voice in the sacred
name of life together with all
the gifts of unity, justice and
peace.

CHURCH

the last walk down second avenue
led me to the old church where I
entered with my gospel of a lynched
peasant who read scriptures that did
not have a single white person in it
and never heard a word of American
English. the congregation smug with
feelings of election looked sideways
at me denying the possibility that a
blessed encounter could come in the
form of a spic on their upscale pew.
God bless the fundamentalist, liberals
and the whole motley crew in that fine
church that never scattered love on the
streets and is endowed with theological
discredit. I stayed the hour departing just
seconds before the closing prayer ended
and just in time for my crucified God to
put enough balm over my wounds to let
me keep walking to get living done and
try the best I could to recall Jesus weeps
for them, too.

A PARABLE

the luxury places uptown
forbid loitering by beggars
on their fine steps and the
poor who mop the floors
and haul rubbish beyond the
condo doors are overlooked
like judgement day is not a
breath away. the tiny pocket
Bible Lela brings to work to
read the stories of Moses and
the prophets never did mean
a damn thing to the rich man
who licks his fingers at a table
of splendor hunched over each
dish like a gluttonous old fool
unaware of his afflictions. one
day the beggars on the street, like
Lela will pass into a world that
belongs exclusively to God, the
garden of peace, a place released
from want, illness, indifference
and hate. one day these overlooked
people full of sores will be carried
by Angels to the bosom of Abraham
to enjoy an everlasting feast, while
the rich upper east side man will

fall into an abyss with flames no
anguish can ever quell. one day
the rich man will beg Lela, the
beggars and all the people scorned
by indifferent wealth to spare a few
drops of water from heaven to stop
the burning on his loathing tongue
that finally from hell begs. the people
that in tears were never given bread
weep no more and God knows them
by name but the nameless rich man
must now face an eternity of woe!

THANKSGIVING

what will you do with this
precious day? will you give
thanks with enormously wide
eyes like the still green trees,
birds in flight, the dreamy blue
sky and the softly blowing wind?
what will you do with new dreams,
the tastes, smells, sounds and sights
of life awake? what will you do beneath
the warming sun, the daily trials and the
deep stirring within?   listen, you may
confess each moment a prayer and give
thanks for every answer waving in the
dark that makes us all stumble.

THE CRYING

the people ranting free who
are known to the world by
the quality of their doubt and
maddening ways are having
a day blowing the noise of
conspiracy themes and other
spawns of idiocy into a world
imprisoned by illness. hostile
to the ways of reason and glad
to vilify the accomplishment of
science they would have us live
in their illusions and throw fetid
lines of nonsense at the medicine
keeping us from an early grave on
earth. what does all their blabbing
say they know of life? what do they
know of things divine like science
dropped like proofs, measures and
mystical sweet breezes from heaven
with loud applause for living? those with
fractured brains eluding scientific light
please think hard, long and deeply
before you say more foolish words
that even the intoxicating realms of
common sense find pitiful.

THE SIDEWALK

on the sidewalk, boys play handball
against the grocery store wall, girls
still find ways to skip rope till dark,
priests walk beside the neighborhood
drunks, students stroll home uniformed
from Catholic school and the harlot who
was baptized in St. John's Church smiles
below the low still clouds. when you close
your eyes, the rustling leaves from the single
tree in the middle of the block makes sounds
like a rumbling forest that exchanges dreams
with the people who live here. new arrivals
are not forgotten in these parts just north of
Manhattan island that we have seen floating
in fog and together we are fit for the highest
prizes of Spanglish town and the wonderfully
mystical benediction that one day will drop
on us from heaven.

NOISE

on a misty
night
when sirens
howled
down
the dark street
with
noise
louder
than mine,
I sat
thinking
of home
and
fixed
on the
lights
in windows
across
the
avenue
from
the
place
where I
yearned
for
warmth.

ABSURD DEMOCRACY

tonight, I will go to the near empty
street where a television plays in a
shop window with captions on the
screen popping ideas that lick the
brains of those who spend days
walking in their sleep occupied with
conspiracy theories that recreate the
world in folly and slowly murder the
innocent who measure their lives
with dreams. I have known the people
gasping for air, the voices never heard,
the dark eyes full of tears and the ragged
claws scratching out with ugly fingers
the truth. tonight, I will stand by the
shop window with others staring at the
screen refusing to have scales put on my
eyes, aware of the odor of absurdity that
lingers on the streets, towns, cities and
the halls of Congress where the elected
are redoubled with deceit and criminals
get away with what lefty who is in prison
for stealing a car battery would never in
a thousand years imagine. tonight, I will
stand with the pitiless in a country rushing
to undo itself with human idiocy, disgraced
tyrants and respectable elected officials

who know too little about disassembling
the bullshit killing children and keeping
offenders free.

GIMBELS

Gimbel's department store
in New York was a magnet
in the 60s for city kids who
loved to show up downtown
to roam its floors where white
men with scant hair and fancy
suits kept watch. middle-aged
women sailed in from Herald
Square escaping the December
cold winds with eyes the Puerto
Rican kids from the Bronx did
not understand and with snow
white made-up faces. we walked
the floors with collegians, maids,
laborers, priests, well-dressed old
men and careless faced little white
kids held by the hand. we made our
way to the toy department like boys
on a treasure hunt full of marvel in
the downtown world, trying our best
not to be eaten by the security guards,
bewitched by bright lights and the strong
smells of newness and delighted to have
the Spanglish blues in us held completely
still. we saw them for the first time in that
store, the rock-and-sock them robots, no

one could buy but we invented a sacred
story about them on the long subway ride
home and took refuge in it.

CARAVAN

life on the other side of
the border is not without
tears. you can hear how it
announces itself when the
children cross in the arms
of tired mothers with hope
wider than the world. what
you heard is true about the
devastating violence, the terror
children act on children, the
brutality of the prophets of hate,
the legs tossed in ravens, torsos
without heads, and teeth kept
for trophies from a civil war
paid for by U.S. tax dollars and
today delivered by the tattooed
faces of youth with guns that dish
out the same death tickets. I have
walked many miles in a martyred
country that killed bishops, nuns,
pastors, priests and the poor and
fell to my knees in tears hearing
that the thirteen-year-old girl we
looked for was decapitated on an
empty street of this Godless republic
still making the sign of the cross. even

now, I can hear chains rattling in our
hearts that God has not yet broken and
churches still waiting

DEATH

death calls us by name
to end a story in lightless

places. it shows up at the
oddest time with soundless

eagerness and leaves pale
conversations behind. it

is a visitor dishing out a
slap on the face, the one

holding us in an eternal
grip and listening closely to

the last words spoken in our
own tongue. death knows the

mourners parading on the streets
and it pretends not to hear the

prayers of the faithful that guide
the departed to the sweet gate of

heaven with a brand-new set of
keys to enter the land of never

ending saintly wandering.

THE LIE

we live in an exceptional country
that goes extra miles to wash the

truth. this word is rejected, despised
and even when handed to us from

heaven denied. truth cannot walk
the streets without a helmet for it

will be pounced on like protesters
in a Black Lives Matter march,

women demanding equal rights
or migrants hollering to be let out

of cages in the name of the great
cause of mercy, justice and love.

we live in a unique nation where
blindfolded citizens afraid of a colorful

world dissolve in their narrow minds
truth like rain washing away footsteps

in sand. we live in a society with too many
citizens who kill for lies, never tell each

other what we know and soil the flag with
innocent blood. we live in a republic that

protects fabrications, moves forward with
deception and stomps on people who have

the nerve to raise questions. I tell you there
is a difference between those who dream

and those who bolt the door, human beings
and monsters, the cross and nails, truth and

the fully grown sham.

COME, HOLY SPIRIT

I sit on the building steps
whispering come Holy Spirit
waving from a window on the
cross town bus, bring us news
from anywhere on earth of the
crippled, the blind, or the meek
you have left with signs. Come,
Holy Spirit whatever you happen
to be and lean into the weeping
world full of people that marvel
about the tales of you they read
in ancient books and guided hands
writing testimonies.

MY PEOPLE

for those who live on the
hyphen wondering about

the next step's direction,
listening to voices on all

sides insisting one remain
midway to nowhere, each

day lived searching for a
dream to indulge just enough

to call one's own and always
standing on the thin line of

America that keeps one in a
raging silence. for those who

wake up each day afraid, hear
the rumbling in the hungry

stomachs of thinning kids, are
unwelcomed in the cities set

upon the hills and collide with
the complexities of a prison

entirely made with white sheets.
for those with words of instruction

about what it means to be human,
who push through the closed doors,

have daily flings with mercy and
hope, you will taste the sweetest

portions of sacred bread that will
make you smile like people who

yet live.

LOOK UP

I know this peace will not
last too long, the aches are
working their way around
our bones, the bitter sighs
yet play in our ears, our dark
hands sign the fires next time
and wounds go on seeking a
place with healing balm that
is better than a nation full of
pitiful white hate. I know
no matter what, we will sit
with these American made
scars and find time to have
a look at the stars with that
stubborn insistence made of
freedom thoughts that the
chariots are coming.

CROSSING OVER

on this side of the line that
separates different speaking

worlds the land she first saw
in magazines and Kellogg's

cereal boxes is not the place
she believed for rest. she is

cast off daily, scarcely known
by the country that has forgotten

to show kindness to strangers,
still fleeing in her head gangs

that do not spare kids and
afraid of not being in a safer

country. in the church with
candles illuminating all the

dark corners, priests drawing
water from their wells offered

to quench her thirst, too few
believe her terrible stories of

violence committed by mafias
of the poor. after putting her

child to bed at night, she sits
wondering now that Romero

is gone who is there for her,
feels with her, and weeps with

her over the names of everyone
dead? she often wails too bad

God did not cross the border with
me into the English-speaking world

disguised with the ornaments of
an aging faith!

LONG WAY

coming this long way to
New York City you found

delight playing in the first
snow and in the tiny flakes

gently falling to earth. you had
never seen streets covered

in a sheet of white, thrown
snowballs at a passing bus

or experienced the spell of
winter quite the same way in

your gracefully sun-warmed
Spanish speaking world. yet,

on cold mornings off to work
sweeping offices downtown

you long for home, the sound
of birds' glad songs in a forest,

church bells ringing long and
loud and Spanish shedding her

melodious charms on village
streets lined for blocks with

colorfully painted walls. in a
few years, when your children

run home from school excited
about reading English speaking

stories in books you will know
the secret charms of the dream

that brought you to a Northern
and faraway shore.

THE MARTYRS

in the corridors the cross did
hang where soldiers entered
priests' rooms to split open
their heads with viciousness
so far from God. for those
with eyes that cry and hearts
that grieve these University
martyrs are the beggars on
the Cathedral steps, abuelas
saying goodbye to sons and
daughters heading North, the
campesinos on the mountain
side picking coffee for the
accumulators of wealth, the
unemployed, hungry children,
the blessed poor imprisoned,
murdered, raped and trashed
by the world that makes death.
today, we remember the Jesuit
martyrs, their cook and her teen
daughter whose violent deaths
give us life, we recall their sacred
witness in the gardens where we
cry and smile at the sound of the
distant church bells still ringing.

today, we remember, pray, weep,
speak and rejoice for these our
precious martyrs will never be
silenced!

THE GRAVES

Lord, you may hear the earthly
weeping and see your marvelous
light darkened by the heartless
judges who are tangled in lies,
crowned with white stupidity
and driven to keep racist wheels
in motion. Lord, undoing justice
is a national pass time belonging
to the people who say the rope
they carry over their shoulders
and the AR-15 in the hands of
white teens terrifyingly paraded
on the racial protest streets proves
only a motivation for self-defense.
Lord, you may understand today
why many of us live in a state of
permanent rage putting up with the
manipulations of the rule of law
making white supremacists shine
like the innocent and allowing them
to stand on the sinking earth of too
many cemeteries with their sardonic
grin. Lord, you know very well it
is time to tell history backward in
America about the weeping and dying

of middle passage and the slaughtered
Black lives you have seen for years on
the brutalizing shores of a nation not
right with you.

THANKSGIVING DAY

we never went to the Macy's
Thanksgiving Day Parade to
see the floats and marching
bands in step. on the stoops
the brown bodies exchanged
stories of the smallest things
that ever happened for which
to be thankful and whether the
unspoken mysteries of heaven
would soar above the marchers
downtown with God not looking
away. it never mattered that no
one had an extravagant turkey feast
and climbing up five flights of
steps to eat with an old woman
everyone called abuela was for us
the journey across the river and
through the words. we never gave
a thought about being poor in a rich
city, managed somehow on this feast
day to feel unblemished by the wrong
that pushed mothers and fathers into
a strange new world, recited together
thankful prayers in Spanish and saw
each other's glad faces.

MORNING

this morning the wind is blowing
cold, the sky is dense with greyish

clouds, the trees appear a little more
bent and I can almost hear the people

on the block who awake from sleep
hoping this gentle time will offer them

a sign of their purest dreams. I see the
old women strolling on the sidewalk to

begin their hours full of direction, not
talking of the things that have happened

to them in the years of living and bathed
in heavenly light. the Viejo just came

out of an alley pulling a two-wheeled
cart toward Southern Boulevard filled

with different sized umbrellas that he
will sell cheaply to people afraid of the

possibility of thrashing rain and he will
be out on the corner until the pale moon

comes to whisper it's time to go. there
goes Tito who wakes up at the snap of

dawn waiting again for the Holy Spirit
to come through the cracks in the building

bricks, sitting quietly in the departing dark
before dashing out to catch a subway ride

downtown to a law firm where he works
in a mailroom always a stranger. these souls

purify the sacred words I sometimes hear in
aging churches, while disclosing to me the

deepest mysteries of love.

STREETS KIDS

this kid's mother died in a
clandestine jail when rich
people set the army loose
on the poor. he ran away
with his father whose name
is tattooed in bold letters on
his dark-skinned back, after
he was killed on the street.
there is no way to tell how
many like him will grow into
a new life, get rounded up in
an ICE raid or murdered in the
name of the barrio's narcotic
charms. the trumpets he says
are not blowing loud enough
for Jesus to come to the world
that just lets kids die.

THE WEDDING

this union out of a whole
life has come today with

love. in this gracious light
we saw two hearts at peace

with heaven's tenderness
pouring in whether by ear,

eye or soul. we came from
far and near to linger in this

place gathering the scent of
the beautiful, gladness that

never ends and the delicious
paradise hour by hour we dare

not dream. we saw two darlings
in the clear light of early evening

threaded with the miracles that
connect the stars and ensures the

earth rolls beneath our feet. today,
love issued radiant from the altar,

the sand from different shores, the
uniting rings and taken hands that

in their gentle way pointed to the
years that will bend with aging

when you each will declare: I have
loved you before eternity and now

more deeply wandering this sweet
earth.

THE CHOIR

they showed up in small groups
every ten minutes filling the
pews a row at a time and the
walls of the church were lined
with portraits of the martyrs
who gave their lives for the smallest
country in Latin America and all the
poor. cracked paint, broken windows,
a rod iron fence, ants walking circles
on the sanctuary steps experienced the
priest's Sunday blessings drawing them
a little closer to life. young musicians
gathered in a corner before a picture of
San Oscar Romero, pitching their concert
A behind masked faces displaying hope in
their eyes. a girl in love in the second pew
with eager ears listened to the spiritual that
trembled up the aisles of the little church that
leaves the lights on at night. the youthful
choir that morning had no power to ease
hard times, the weight of crooked years nor
sweet days that died but every second in song
lulled us into the space of wondrous things to
make us turn to whisper to each other God
what singers!

DAVID (R.I.P.)

the students in the school
yet dream to move lightly
on their feet, smoothly across
the training floor, elegant with
body lines to make and recalling
the needs of grace. the voices at
the studio, in their homes, in the
places that see us pray and memory
keeps awake will not allow your
light to go out though sadness has
crept into them. together we say,
you fair friend will never part these
broken hearts that watched you turn
the corner, we will look for you on
the mortal paths beneath the moon's
pale light, the lanes yet warmed by the
rays of a gentle Sun, when looking up
at the lengthening blue sky and hearing
mourning doves sing. we have spent the
last few days breathless, reading soundless
words from last week's newspaper, hearing
the ancient church bells ringing out your
name from somewhere and you whispering
to us from your vertical journey come closer
and feel this peace.

THE RESURRECTED

today you may say with
your twisted hate that my

Brown Spanglish life is not
worth a dime. you may try

to prevent every step taken
by my beautiful dark people

entering a new life. you may
attempt with your hopeless

violence to pound us into the
earth your people stole and

make us hemorrhage the way
for centuries you filled rivers

with Black blood. your small
mind cannot understand hope

will never end for us and your
nights of terror will be measured

for hundreds of years by every
mockingbird's song. today, you

may look at us with not a single
word of praise for your creator

in heaven who made us beautiful
and with dark skin. today, you will

learn we possess an ancient love that
is Black, Brown, differently tongued

and always resurrecting.

THE DARK

I have many memories fired
in the dark in familiar seasons

of struggle that on mountains
erupt like images that come to

one at the end of a life. they
are stories given to me by the

poor fiercely describing fresh
new ways to hope and live in

a loathing world. I have known
too many campesinos here who

weep until death departs them.
they waited for new days to come,

for love to be carried into the
world with Angel's wings, for

reasons that point to change
no one would find unworthy

and to drift a little closer to love
and justice. I have learned to carry

the future for them, to find it in Bibles,
reciting prayers in Spanish, delighting

in the life of school children gloated
with dreams and hearing the voices

of those gone yet whispering in the
dark to me. I confess the people of

corn who walk in the dark are right,
one day lightening will slice the top

of government and God will begin
a new heaven on earth!

UKRAINE

we see the bloody streets,
empty squares, wide holes

on buildings and hear the
cries of the orphaned, the

elderly, the frightened and
confused that rises to God

in heaven. we sense the grief
of Ukraine for the dead that

only makes the coffin makers
weep. another tyrant's story

will be added to the pages of
history, lessons will be taught

by the little ones once grown
up in schools, pictures from the

places manufactured by Putin's
crimes will be shown and new

monuments will be raised to pay
tribute to those who resisted the

Herodian thug hell bent on toppling
a Ukrainian Jew who leads a country

older than Russia. some in the world
choose murderous ways and graveyards

for the innocent but these barbarians
will never have the last word which

belongs to the victims of incalculable
war crimes who love their freedom

and life.

AMEN

I will travel far come morning
when the dark shakes me awake,
the world sleeps with dreams and
Cassiopeia in the sky sets out to
fade. I will tell stories in the dear
light of an unknown village on a
mountainside about a beloved friend
present in every echo of light in the
dim sanctuary welcoming a lad for
religious confirmation before the eyes
of seasoned coffee pickers, sugar-cane
cutters and distance migrants who know
the ancient ways. I will give thanks for
learning at the last-minute the other side
made room for me, a letter would help
me travel across borders and up the side
of a mountain to hear in the patient hours
of morning incredibly fresh prayers that
turn a ritual experience into a gesture of
love and from that moment forward becomes
a never ending day. I will not forget to say
in the service and with the letter that will
never leave me, amen!

CPSIA information can be obtained
at www.ICGtesting.com
Printed in the USA
LVHW080500191022
731046LV00008B/296